HARMONY
IN YOUR CAREER
& IN YOUR SOUL

FINDING
YOUR ULTIMATE
FULFILLMENT
FROM THE
INSIDE OUT

DONNA R. STYER & SCOTT B. MCNELIS

Styer, Donna R.
Harmony in your career and in your soul
ISBN: 978-1-64649-241-1 (paperback)
ISBN: 978-1-64649-242-8 (ebook)
1. Conduct of life.   2. Vocational guidance.
3. Self-realization.   I. McNelis, Scott B.
II. Title. BJ1581.2.S79 2000   158.1C00-911218-9

Second Edition

 Year of the Book Press
135 Glen Ave
Glen Rock, PA 17327

Printed in the United States

Dedication

I dedicate this book in loving memory to the courageous women in my family, especially my Mother, Geraldine M. Styer. May she forever stand tall.

—Donna R. Styer

DEDICATION

This book is dedicated to the many people who have blessed my life with love, understanding, and wisdom. Most of all, I dedicate this to my wife, Lisa, and my daughters, Kiernan and Brynne, who are models of pure faith and love.

—Scott B. McNelis

ACKNOWLEDGMENTS

We want to thank our publisher, Demi Stevens, for her insightful enhancements, and our graphic artist, Chris Loretz, for his creativity and patience with our numerous revisions. Also, thanks to Joanne Young-Stephan, a lettering artist who greatly enhanced the look of our project, as well as Judy Sammett for assistance on the development of our charts. We thank Lori Stahl, Cindi Dixon, and Jonathan Elder for their fine photography. A very special thanks to our administrative assistant, Caryn Andes of A.S.A.P. She has been so patient and understanding. Thank you, Caryn! In addition, thanks to author Carole Turkington for her advice and guidance as we navigated through our project.

And from Donna...

I would like to thank my wonderful clients past, present, and future who shared their career dreams and goals with me. You have all been most inspirational in my career.

A heartfelt thank you to my loving and supportive family and my very special friends. Your presence in my life is a true blessing!

CONTENTS

FOREWORD

This book is a pure collaboration between two people who share the passion to assist others in their search for more fulfilling careers. The path from concept to completion of this project flowed well as we worked together.

Harmony In Your Career & In Your Soul is about finding a meaningful place in the world of work... a career that resonates with who you are, so much that it does not seem like work. We know this feeling well and we were fortunate to have this experience as we collaborated on this project. It has been an exciting journey, filled with ideas and creativity. The flow we created was authentic and natural. This book encourages the same for you in your search for a more fulfilling career.

Throughout this book, gender-specific terms may be used in order to ease the text flow. Whenever a gender-specific term is used, it should be understood as referring to all genders and gender identities, unless explicitly stated. This is done solely for the purpose of making the text easier to read, and no offense or sexism is intended.

INTRODUCTION

Achieving harmony in your career and in your soul is a journey that begins from the "inside," by paying attention to values, dreams, goals, talents, and desires.

Yet many people only listen to "outside" voices of expectations and circumstances. They may have material success, but they are disillusioned by the realities of their work.

Those people are discovering what you already know— that *success without satisfaction* is not good enough! In fact, studies have shown that at least 56% of individuals would like to change positions. Studies have also shown that doing what you love has a positive physiological effect.

Yet changing careers can be terrifying. Better to stick with what's safe than risk failure, right?

Wrong!

During my years as a professional career coach, I have helped hundreds of people just like you. My experience has taught me these things:

- Many choose careers for the wrong reasons.

- Career success without satisfaction is not enough. You spend 40 hours a week or more at your job.

It is important to do something that feeds your soul as well as your wallet.

- A career change doesn't have to be scary. I've devised an approach where dilution is part of the solution. It lets you try out new options without burning bridges.

My clients urged me to write this book. They say most career guides out there offer a high-stress mix of job-hunting advice and goal-oriented cheerleading. They don't tell you how to look within yourself and find the career that's right for you. What my clients wanted was a guide they could turn to again and again for insight and affirmation.

This book is unique because I understand your needs for career fulfillment, and I believe you can get there—authentically! The process I share with you fosters a return to your *core self* in a very simple and clear format. I have experienced enormous success with my clients through this approach, and I am delighted to share it with you.

Harmony In Your Career & In Your Soul is filled with gentle holistic advice and real-life examples from people I have coached. Many clients wait until they've reached a crisis point before they see me. But you can act before that.

If you feel unfulfilled and frustrated, but terrified of change, think of this book as a gift to yourself. It will help you move toward a greater understanding of where you belong in the world of work and ultimately guide you to greater career fulfillment.

~1~

MY JOURNEY TO CAREER SATISFACTION

"The present moment is a powerful Goddess."
—Goethe

People who have career satisfaction look forward to going to work each day. In fact, they don't really think of it as work—their careers are more like natural expressions of their authentic selves.

But in my years as a professional coach, I've met hundreds of people who head to their offices each morning with feelings of anger, dread, or disappointment. Some dislike their bosses, others feel overwhelmed by paperwork, and still others are just bored and unchallenged with the daily grind. Also, they are looking to achieve a work/life balance.

I know how they feel. I was an executive at a large telecommunications company. Some days, when I put on my corporate suit, I felt like I was putting on a costume, one that forced me to suppress my true personality and abilities behind a structure that wasn't right for me.

All those meetings and sales quotas were stifling a creative side that was just begging to come out. But big corporations have specific ways of doing things and new ideas are not always popular.

I coped with this lack of fulfillment for several years, lulled by the security of a steady paycheck. But eventually I realized my own joy and contentment were more valuable than all the money in the world. I knew I had to resign.

When I finally left my job, I wasn't sure exactly what I would do. But I was determined to find something that would resonate with my being, work that felt connected to my soul.

I initially joined a recruiting business, and I just loved it. After my own experience of following the wrong career path, I got tremendous joy out of helping people make the right career choices!

Within a year, I started my own consulting business, and soon many other services were added, including management consulting, training, career counseling, and professional coaching. Every day, I love what I do. It doesn't seem like work, just a part of who I am.

This book can help you find the same career satisfaction. So let's start your journey toward the refinement and realization of your career goals.

~2~
LUKE'S STORY

"I learn by going where I have to go."
—Theodore Roethke

This is a good time to introduce you to one of my clients and explain how my gentle career philosophy worked for him. Here is his story.

Luke had been a minister for 25 years, and he was both liked and respected. He came from a long line of ministers and had never thought about doing anything else.

But the day-to-day stresses of the job were tearing him apart. By the time he came to me, he was convinced he could not perform his job one more day. He felt depressed and ineffective.

The ministry, of course, is an extremely service-oriented field. Luke was on call day and night, handling the problems and crises of his many parishioners.

When he wasn't working, he was spending time with his wife and children. Consequently, he had little time for himself. His personal interests had been pushed aside for so long he really had no place to go for renewal.

3

I suggested to Luke that he give himself something he had not been able to get anyplace else—permission to explore his own desires and motivations.

Together we concluded that it was okay to be tired of what he was doing and together we gave him permission to leave his job at any time. He was greatly relieved to share his thoughts with someone who understood and heard him.

Our conversation was very liberating for Luke who was worried that a career change would disappoint his elderly parents and also disrupt his sense of security.

He confided that he enjoyed boating, nature, and golf, but felt he had no time for those activities. The more we discussed his interests, the more I saw the signs of stress leave his face and body. By the third or fourth session, his hunched posture and tight facial expression had eased.

Our goal over the next few months was to restore some work/life balance to Luke's life.

I don't mean I told Luke to become self-absorbed. I simply emphasized that he needed to take better care of himself. I reminded him that an adult who has no control over his life doesn't really have his own life—it belongs to other people.

As with many of my clients, the solution for Luke was remarkably simple. From our discussions, he realized that the work wasn't the problem. His problem was an inability to create boundaries.

Luke kept his job and he added staff to help him with his workload. Now he has more time to explore his own interests, and he feels a renewed sense of job satisfaction.

The key for Luke was giving himself permission to explore his options. Many of my clients feel trapped in careers that satisfy the wallet but not the soul.

In the following chapters, we'll discuss why many of us do things we don't really enjoy, and we'll discuss ways to break out of those traps.

~3~
HOW DID THIS HAPPEN TO ME?

"I found a space in all the noise...
and listened to the silence."
—Anon

Luke, like many people, follow a particular career path because of external pressures—in his case, a family history. Most people starting their professional life or considering a career change make the same mistake. They look all around them—they ask friends for advice, read about the latest career trends, and maybe look in the classified ads for inspiration.

We're going to take a different approach and begin your journey toward career satisfaction by looking within. So find a place without distractions, and listen to your inner voice as you take the following quiz.

WELCOME TO THE PROCESS!
The following process will help you uncover your deepest thoughts and wishes about the type of work you want to do. These ideas will be further refined in later chapters.

To fully reap the benefits of this process, it's important to adhere to the following ground rules:

Rule #1: Reject limitations. Accept that all of your dreams are possible in some form or another.

Rule #2: Be positive about your richest resource—*you!* Give yourself the gift of trying, and know that it's never too late to try. Acknowledge your natural talents and special skills!

Rule #3: Do not hold back. If you cannot accept some of your new ideas, try to gently and gradually accept them for a while, until they seem more acceptable. The results of this exercise do not have to be shared with anyone.

Let's get started! The only materials you need are you and some means to record your answers to the questions. Paper and pen or a recorder will usually do the trick.

Find a quiet place without distractions. Give yourself time without any interruptions. Get comfortable. If soothing background music relaxes you—go for it! Listen to the sound of your breathing... just you alone with your thoughts and dreams. Relax...

Remember there are no incorrect answers!

QUESTIONS

Take a moment to look in the mirror. What do you see?

What do your eyes say about you?

What would you like your eyes to say about you?

How would people describe you? Is that how you see yourself? Contrast all differences, if possible.

If you had to draw a picture of all of the things happening in your life around you, what would it look like? You may draw the picture if you like. If you can't draw, that's OK. Stick figures are great.

If you had to draw a picture of all of the feelings inside you, what would you draw? You may draw the picture if you like.

What is your objective today?

What do you believe are your greatest strengths?

What do you do to find joy and relaxation? How do you spend your leisure time? Do these activities help you take care of yourself?

Imagine. If you could do anything you wanted for the rest of your life, what would it be? Describe it in as much detail as possible... when, where, how, and with whom? You may draw the scenes if you wish. Remember there are no limitations!

When do you feel the most content? Most alive?

What steps have you taken to move toward this dream or to experience some aspects of this dream?

YOUR PRIORITIES

Looking at the following list of career values, assign priorities of 1 to 5, with 1 being the highest ranking and 5 as the lowest. If you have additional values than shown below, add them to the list.

_____ Financial compensation
_____ Geographic location
_____ Fringe benefits of the job
_____ Role and scope of the work match true interests
_____ People you work with
_____ Opportunity for advancement
_____ An environment that encourages and rewards empowerment
_____ Positive feedback on the job from co-workers and leaders
_____ Career planning, evolution on paths to success
_____ Personal satisfaction from the work
_____ Flexible work schedule/remote opportunities
_____ Work/Life balance
_____ Others (please list)

When was the last time you complimented a co-worker? What did you say?

When was the last time you complimented a friend? What did you say?

When was the last time you complimented a child? What did you say?

When was the last time you complimented yourself? What did you say?

Take a moment and list five compliments to yourself. I know you can do it!

Congratulations! You have just given yourself many special gifts: time to know how you are feeling at this moment, a current perception of yourself, insights into where you might like to go, and affirmations of the many natural talents and skills that you possess. Not bad for just a bit of quiet time!

As we progress through this book, you will learn how to apply your new awareness of self on your journey to create your career path. Along the way, remember to tell yourself what you like about you, and remind yourself of all of the things you do best! Continue to think of times when you feel filled with enthusiasm, joy, and contentment.

P.S. You may have felt a little uneasy complimenting yourself. If so, you are not alone. Although most people are willing to compliment others, they are uncomfortable granting the same favor to themselves. Perhaps we all learned that doing so would seem conceited.

If you feel that way, I suggest you approach complimenting yourself as just another way to self-affirm you and your talents and recognize your value to yourself and others. You are wonderful and unique!

~4~

PEOPLE COME IN ALL SHAPES AND SIZES

"It always comes back to the same necessity:
go deep enough and there is a bedrock of
truth, however hard." —May Sarton

During my years as a career coach, I have worked with many diverse and talented people who have come to the conclusion that change in their career path is necessary.

A very exciting part of my job is helping them gain an awareness of their feelings regarding their work. We discuss, in depth, what they like and dislike about their jobs.

After working with me, many clients decide to move in new career directions. Some leave their jobs and some find ways to gain more pleasure from their existing careers, or they decide to change jobs within their current company.

Some of my clients feel trapped—as if they have nowhere to turn. Sometimes, I guess, I'm the last resort! My objective is for them to give themselves permission to consider their career alternatives and uncover what they might really like to do. It is okay to be tired of what you are doing or the way you are doing it. I help them focus. This world is filled with wonderful opportunities.

I tell them to list their top five priorities for a career. Do they crave personal satisfaction? Is flexibility important? Maybe they want to make a certain amount of money. The next step is putting these priorities in order.

Sometimes clients report that they feel "numb" in their current work situations. These people have spent a large part of their career feeling stale and unchallenged and they yearn for greater career satisfaction.

"Angry victims" are another group of clients who are motivated to change jobs for different reasons than the earlier categories.

One client I remember from this category stomped into my office, shook my hand gruffly, did not smile, and plopped himself down in one of my chairs.

It turned out that he was recently passed over for a job that would have involved much more customer contact for the company. "They say I am not polished enough at this point," he blurted out. As we talked, and the color of his face deepened from rosy to a scarlet hue, I realized that this guy was mad at his boss, wife, parents, and kids.

Over the next few weeks, we discovered innumerable layers of anger. I allowed him to purge his feelings until we were ready to discuss a rational course of action.

The answer for him was to handle his anger productively and grow from it. Ultimately, he stayed in the same line of work but took a position with another company to experience a fresh start with his newfound knowledge of self.

Sometimes a client's distress comes not from the actual work, but from the way he or she perceives and manages it.

People in this category may enjoy the work they are doing, however, they feel they must leave their current employer. One of my primary objectives in a circumstance such as this, is to allow the client to understand his or her anger. I suggest ways for him or her to cope until they find other employment or help them see that a sense of detachment may help them cope better and continue to do the work they like to do.

The final category of clients is what I term the "impatient" clients. These people tend to have a very high opinion of their abilities and are seeking immediate gratification. I had a client recently who focused primarily on financial compensation and prestige. When I suggested he think about job satisfaction and the long-term benefits of enjoying his work, it stopped him dead in his tracks. He had not thought about the price one pays for simply a monetary reward.

~5~

YOUR DREAMS ARE WORTH KEEPING

---

*"The future belongs to those who
believe in the beauty of their dreams."
—Eleanor Roosevelt*

Dreams... they have a unique way of telling us what we need to know. They help us understand our wishes for the future and remind us of the fears that keep us from turning those wishes into realities.

I'm not just talking about the dreams that come to us when we're sleeping. Dreams also include daydreams, visions, desires, and the little voices inside all of us (also known as intuition) that suggest ways to make our lives better. In the next few chapters, we'll give your dreams the attention they deserve. Your dreams are important guides to career satisfaction.

At this point, if you are thinking, "I can't," then I ask you to give yourself the gift of saying, "I will try to make my dreams come true." Allow yourself to believe in your dreams and your vast potential.

~6~

THE SEEDS OF A DREAM

---

*"Whatever you can do
or dream you can do, begin it;
boldness has genius, power,
and magic in it."*
—Goethe

I know many people who have used their ideas as tiny seeds, and, in time, the seeds germinated and became an apparent part of their realities.

One client I worked with, Peter, decided he would be moving to a new job within the company during the year. He came back from Christmas vacation and cleaned his office until it was streamlined and organized. These changes would make it easier for someone else to transition into his job. As he worked on his office, he became more aware that he welcomed change. He felt light and open to new learning opportunities and challenges within his organization. Within two months, he was offered a challenging cross-training assignment which he eagerly accepted.

He left his previous position in a state of readiness and believing in possibilities, largely because he was receptive to the possibility of change in his life.

~7~

WHAT ARE YOUR DREAMS?

"Be still and know."
—Dr. Wayne Dyer

"What are my dreams?" For some of us, this is a very easy question to answer. For others, the response might be, "I'm not sure of my dreams or if I even have any," or, "Who has time to think about dreams? I'm too busy trying to meet all of my responsibilities every day."

The next exercise will reacquaint you with your thoughts and memories about your dreams. Take some time to answer these questions. Please note that I didn't provide examples because I don't want to influence your thoughts with dreams from other people.

THE DREAM EXERCISE

Can you think of a dream or a goal that you had as a child that you expressed and did not receive encouragement, prompting you to abandon the dream? Or perhaps it was *simply pruned out* of you over the years.

Did you ever return to the dream? Does any or all of it creep into your consciousness today? What feelings do you have surrounding the dream?

Are you pursuing this dream in any form today? If so, how?

If you are not pursuing this dream, what barriers are you allowing to hold you back?

~8~

DREAMING ON SOLID GROUND

*"I have made my world and it is a much
better world than I ever saw outside."*
—*Louise Nevelson*

Sometimes we want to make dreams come true to prove something to others and gain wider acceptance. This sort of behavior is very true of children because they seek love and approval from their parents, and sometimes adults continue to be motivated by this need. We'll explore this concept in more depth later. First, let's examine the root of your dreams.

In general, do you think your dreams are woven to provide you with external approval (approval of others) or are they more directly linked to creation of your internal satisfaction? For example, if you accomplish your dream, will it matter to you how others feel about your accomplishment or will you be satisfied with your feelings about your achievement?

Do you recall any "external approval" dreams? Please list them.

Are you pursuing any of these dreams today? If so, please explain why they are rewarding to you.

Do you have any dreams that are providing you with "internal satisfaction?" If so, what are they?

At this point in your life, which dreams are receiving top priority? Are they more geared toward internal satisfaction or skewed toward external approval?

~9~
WELCOME TO THE WORLD
OF DREAM MODELS

---

*"It is only when we fully exercise our capacities
– when we grow – that we have roots in the
world and feel at home with it." —Eric Hoffer*

I have created two models for you to consider as you evaluate your motivations and goals. By understanding the motives for the choices you make, you may discover that, although you think you have been acting from your heart, other powerful forces may be influencing you. I call the first model the NO SURPRISES way of living.

The NO SURPRISES model fits a group of people who choose the safety of conformity over the option of reaching for new heights. Approval of others is critical to their self-worth; consequently, they mostly choose to adhere to the status quo.

From time to time, they feel frustrated about their lives but are not sure why they feel this way. Fortunately, at least for them, they have mastered the skill of not paying attention to this inner conflict or they have learned to cope with this conflict.

"No Surprises Model"

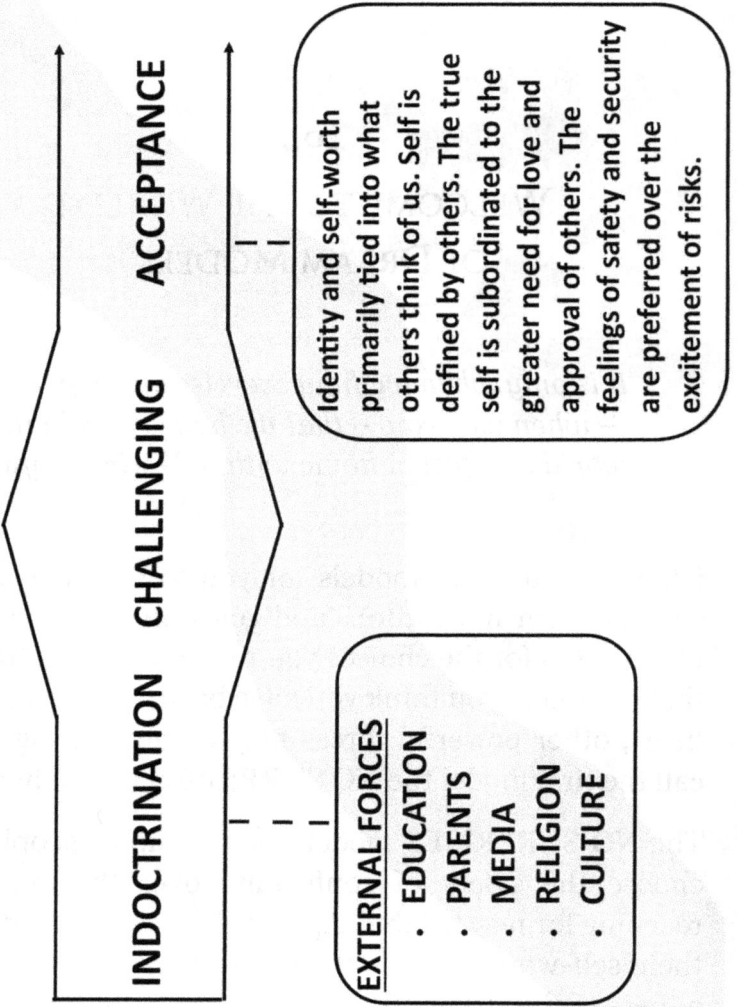

INDOCTRINATION   CHALLENGING   ACCEPTANCE

EXTERNAL FORCES
- EDUCATION
- PARENTS
- MEDIA
- RELIGION
- CULTURE

Identity and self-worth primarily tied into what others think of us. Self is defined by others. The true self is subordinated to the greater need for love and approval of others. The feelings of safety and security are preferred over the excitement of risks.

Under this scenario, dreams certainly do not have much chance of becoming reality. People who fit the NO SURPRISES model accept the status quo. For them this is a comfortable way to live.

In contrast, I have developed the POSSIBILITIES model. People who fit in the POSSIBILITIES model exhibit individuality and adaptability. A person operating under this model respects what has been learned but also challenges these teachings and rules as they relate to how she defines herself.

This individual is able to think outside the box and create meaning in her/his/their life. Dreams play a major role for this person because she/he/they believe in possibilities. This openness allows her to learn new things and have many experiences that will play a factor in her career decision-making.

WE THINK, WE ACT, WE KNOW!

Where do you fall in terms of these models? Do you favor NO SURPRISES or do you believe in POSSIBILITIES? I encourage you to be open to new ideas as you proceed along your career path.

"Possibilities Model"

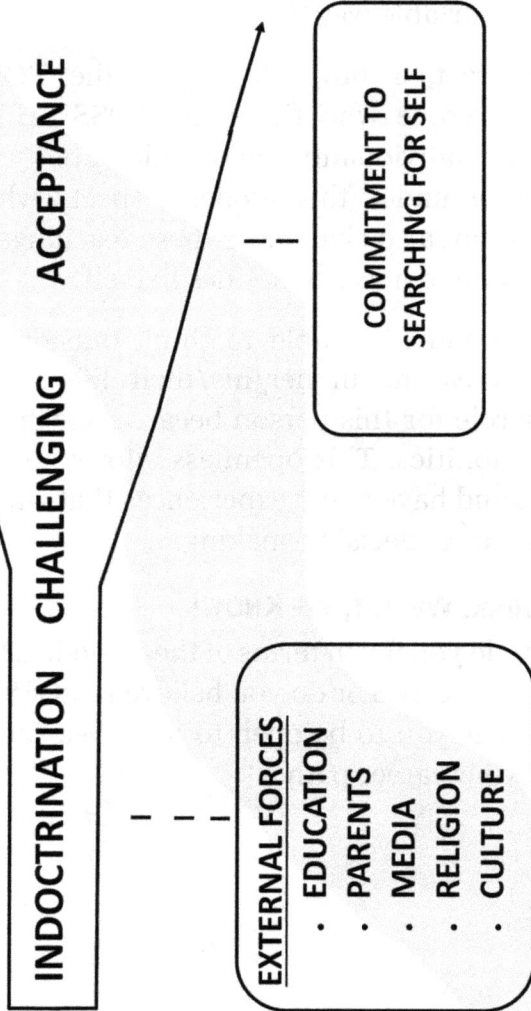

INDOCTRINATION   CHALLENGING   ACCEPTANCE

EXTERNAL FORCES
- EDUCATION
- PARENTS
- MEDIA
- RELIGION
- CULTURE

COMMITMENT TO SEARCHING FOR SELF

~10~
TURNING DREAMS INTO REALITIES

*"Life shrinks or expands
in proportion to one's courage."
—Anais Nin*

Okay, now it's time to get real. We've examined your dreams, and now it's time to show you how to turn them into realities. In the next few chapters, we'll look at the components of your dreamscape, we'll start chipping away at barriers to your goals, and we'll forge ahead with the dreams your heart can't seem to forget.

~11~
BE CAREFUL OF THE WISHING WELL!

"The universe will reward you
for taking risks on its behalf."
—Shakti Gawain

Several years ago, I had the pleasure of meeting a very sweet couple at a dinner. Lauren and Matthew were friendly, and both in their mid-thirties, and had been in the work force for most of their adult lives. We hit it off right away, and they started asking me about the company I worked for and what my position was there.

At the time, I was an upper-level manager in a large corporation.

Prompted by their questions, I described my job in detail. Matthew then told me he wanted to become a corporate manager, too, and he was confident he would get such a job in the very near future. He even asked if any corporate management positions were available in my company.

At this point in the conversation, it was my turn to ask the questions.

I asked Matthew why he thought he would be a good corporate manager. "Because I'm good with people," he replied. As I questioned him further, I learned that he had no education beyond high school and no plans to pursue additional education. He had worked as a customer service representative at a local automobile body shop.

I described to Matthew the typical credentials required for a business management position, including business experience and an education that includes a bachelor's or even a master's degree in business administration.

In addition, I tried to tell him kindly that if he was serious about this career goal, he should start to take the appropriate classes and begin networking in his field of interest.

As I talked, his face grew more and more stern. Finally, he blurted: "I am praying for this career and it will happen for me!"

I am sure the stunned look on my face said many things, but I think he interpreted my expression as reverence for his extreme faith.

Fortunately, we were interrupted by Lauren's announcement that she was going to be a country music star in Nashville. Needless to say, I actually found my cold and ill-prepared banquet dinner more enticing than the remainder of our dinner conversation.

First, let me say that I was not reacting negatively to Lauren and Matthew's desire to pray. Prayer is a wonderful and insightful meditation and can provide clarity around many areas of our lives. However, I was astonished by the vagueness of their goals and their complete unawareness of the preparation required to reach them.

Sadly, as I have come to learn, Lauren and Matthew are not alone in their refusal to take the steps necessary to turn dreams into reality.

In order to make our dreams come true, we must light the fires within ourselves and illuminate our own paths.

~12~
A Look at the Magic Within

---

*"Nothing about human life is more precious
than that we can define our own purpose
and shape our own destiny."*
—Norman Cousins

Somewhere along the line, many of us got the message
that all we had to do was want something badly enough,
and we would get it. Some people buy lottery tickets,
others hope a spouse or child will somehow make their
lives better. These people expect some outside force to
step in and erase their pain.

Many people spend their whole lives wishing and
waiting for that big break. When it doesn't come, they
tell themselves that somehow they were found to be
undeserving. Anger and bitterness follow.

This is a very sad and passive drama. It's even sadder
when people put more energy into this drama than into
making their dreams come true.

In Matthew's case, he was not interested in hearing the
"career active" approach I was describing. Instead, I
believe, he was relying on his community of friends,

family, and acquaintances to produce an opportunity for him.

This is an example of someone relying too much on external resources, sitting back and waiting for something good to happen. Instead of wishing and waiting, Matthew could have been searching his inner self to define the type of career that would meet his needs and be more pro-active in his approach.

It is clear to me that Matthew's approach to finding a career will leave him unfulfilled. I suspect he'll either fall chronically into the "crisis reactive" mode for career change, or he will learn to distrust himself and therefore be afraid to take career risks.

At this point, you may be thinking, "Wow, you're no fun. You don't believe in magic at all!"

Well, that's not true. I do believe in magic. But I believe most of it comes from within ourselves in the form of intuition, thoughts, dreams, visions, ideas, hopes, and apparent coincidences that make us shake our heads in wonder.

This "inner magic" is wonderful and truly serves as the light on our journey toward our dreams. As we move forward in our journey, trust your inner magic to be your guide.

~13~
THE PATH TO YOUR DREAMS

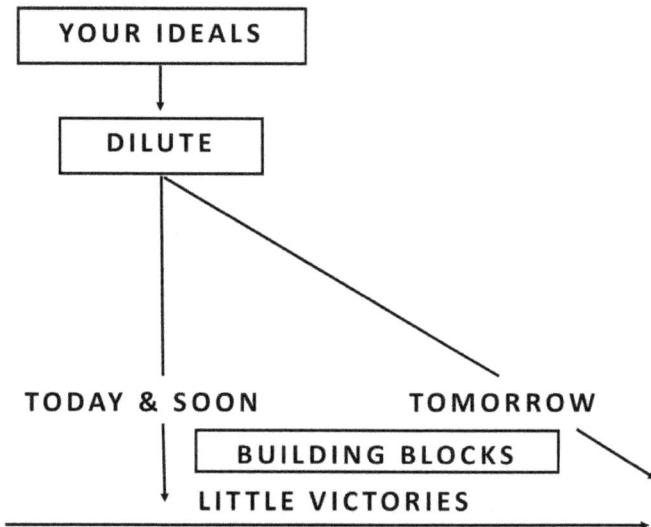

"Our bodies are our gardens,
our wills our gardeners."
—Shakespeare

The purpose of this diagram is to explain the process we are going to explore in the next few pages.

THE PATH TO YOUR DREAMS

```
┌─────────────────┐
│  YOUR IDEALS    │
└─────────────────┘
        │
        ▼
  ┌──────────────┐
  │   DILUTE     │
  └──────────────┘
        │ ╲
        │   ╲
        │     ╲
        │       ╲
        │         ╲
TODAY & SOON      TOMORROW
        │      ┌────────────────────┐  ╲
        │      │  BUILDING BLOCKS   │   ╲
        ▼      └────────────────────┘
        LITTLE VICTORIES
────────────────────────────────────────►
```

Suppose that Matthew truly knew he wanted to be a corporate manager. And let's depart from the story for a moment and assume he is frustrated—his wishful thinking isn't working out the way he planned.

If he came to me for help, I would tell him he can start toward his goal right away. By creating "building blocks," he is sure to reach his goal in some form.

For Matthew, the building blocks might include exploring what it really means to work as a corporate manager. Perhaps he could interview successful corporate managers to identify what skills are necessary.

What else could Matthew do? Well, he could join a local management association, attempt to work toward a management position with his current employer, take classes that would move him toward his goal, attempt to perform freelance consulting in the area of management, apply for an internship, and so on.

As you can see, any of these steps would move him closer to the world of management. And each step closer to his goal would be a victory for him in terms of managing his career.

What if he finds during the process that he does not like management? That would be a victory, too. As we continue to grow along our career path, ongoing refinement is a great side benefit.

~14~
PUTTING THE SOLUTIONS TO WORK

"We lose, only to gain;
we let go, only to receive."
—Gene Clemens

A few years ago, I coached Allison, an accountant who wanted to resign from her job and start her own business. However, she lacked the confidence and financial security to branch out on her own.

She thoroughly enjoyed assisting individuals with their tax returns. I suggested she make a $20 investment in business cards that advertised her ability to prepare income taxes on an as-needed basis.

Within weeks of distributing her new business cards to a small group of people, Allison had several jobs lined up. Those jobs led to others. Her part-time business was in full swing.

The experience was empowering and confidence-building. All she needed was permission to try something outside her routine.

She even remained on her job for some time after developing her tax business because suddenly she had choices and, well, the job was not so bad after all.

As you try these building blocks, belief in yourself is essential.

Recently, I counseled a woman, Elizabeth, who had developed a program for teaching elementary school children the importance of responsibility. Her plan, which drew upon her experiences as a teacher, was impressive. On our first visit, she ran down the specifics, then asked me what I thought.

"Do I have a concept?" she asked.

My response to her was, "Do *you* think you have a concept?"

As our sessions continued, sometimes she came by herself and sometimes with her male friend. It became clear to me that she was allowing him to hold her back. She kept looking to him for guidance and approval, reluctant to act on her ideas without his okay.

The aspect that was so interesting was that her friend had no in-depth experience in the field of education.

Finally, I suggested a meeting without her friend. At that meeting, I pointed out that without her friend's approval she seemed unable to move forward on her concept. On occasion, I have met clients who are looking for permission from someone else rather than simply empowering themselves.

Further conversations revealed that she was raised in an environment that revered the veto power of the man of the house, and she was acting accordingly. In terms of her career, she is now doing a solo act, and to my knowledge is sailing along just fine.

Here's one more example:

Michelle was an accountant at a local company who felt bored and "robotic" in her efforts. She worked with the same people day after day, performing the same routine duties. She sat in the same gray chair all day, surrounded by gray furniture and tan walls.

She yearned to work in a setting that would offer variety and a more colorful environment. She decided to pursue a career in the gardening/flower industry. Her dream was to own a flower business.

Instead of quitting her job, she developed a plan. First, she talked with and observed local gardeners and florists and eventually volunteered. Then she got a part-time weekend job in a local greenhouse and began taking a few horticulture courses at a local community college. Each small step moved her closer to the work she loved.

Today she is an apprentice at a very respected flower shop. The faces of new customers and the blooms of every flower imaginable add personal fulfillment and challenge to her days.

~15~
DILUTION IS PART OF THE SOLUTION

---

*"I merely took the energy it takes to pout
and wrote some blues."*
—*Duke Ellington*

Break down your goal into a reasonable plan. Let's say you want to work in the field of travel and you want to get started today. What kind of opportunities are out there?

- Travel planner/consultant
- Cruise ship team member
- Tour expert/guide
- Blogger to review travel locations/tours
- Developer of tours
- Employment with major airlines

Well, let's scratch travel... you really meant to say "fashion." That's the field for you. So what could you do? How could you get started? You could be a...

- Buyer
- Merchandiser

- Fashion critic
- Designer
- Model
- Fashion event planner/show

You could...

- Work at a fashion café
- Volunteer with organizations that produce fashion shows as fundraisers
- Identify fashion trends for mass merchants of clothing

But what if you are one of those people who have a burning desire to make it in the country music industry? Here are some opportunities for you to become a...

- Performer
- DJ
- Line dancer/caller
- Producer

Or you could...

- Open a country music venue
- Work at a country music radio station
- Review country music/blog
- Become a resident expert on country music

Are you getting the idea? As you can see, there are many ways to begin your journey toward your goal. Take some time to brainstorm your opportunities in your fields of interest (try to limit it to your top three fields of interest at this point).

Field of interest_____

Opportunities:

Field of interest_____

Opportunities:

Field of interest_____

Opportunities:

~16~
SKILLS ON THE SILLS

"What lies behind us, and what lies before us are tiny matters, compared to what lies within us."
—*Anon*

One of the most rewarding aspects of my career coaching practice has been the role in assisting others to light a fire and blaze ahead in the wonderful marriage of harmony in their career and in their soul. Helping people realize they do have options, encouraging them to take control, and watching them take meaningful steps toward career choices instead of "career assignment or occurrence" provides me with great fulfillment.

Sometimes I am saddened by the fact that, today, low self-esteem abounds in epidemic proportions. During many of my initial coaching sessions, I am alarmed by the number of clients who are halfway through their lives and claim they do not know what skills and talents they have to offer in the job market. Frequently, when I ask these clients what skills and talents they are proud of, I see facial expressions ranging from fear to blank stares. And so our work begins....

I can recall numerous initial sessions when I compliment a client with comments such as: "You are an excellent verbal communicator" or "I admire the creative way you put your outfit together." Typical responses include: "Oh, it's nothing" or "Do you really think so?" or "I never considered myself a good communicator."

I am reminded once again that so many of us don't realize our great worth, strengths, and potential!

I help people realize what they have to offer. That's what the following chapters are about—identifying natural talents and skills you already have, and resurrecting the ones you thought you left behind, somewhere on the windowsills, to be accessed only from time to time.

~17~

BEING CREATIVE

"Taking a new step, uttering a new word
is what people fear most."
—*Fyodor Dostoyevsky*

Did you know that 80% of the population say they are not creative? Do you think you are one of these people?

Although you may not have whipped up any wall murals lately and are a little scant on new book ideas, you have been creating solutions to scheduling time conflicts with work, the kids' activities, and your social life. You have found ways to finance these activities and invest for the future to fund more activities and choices. And don't forget, you just repainted the house, selected new carpet, and bought some new furniture. Not to mention that, you're reading this book about creating a new career path and achieving a better fit for yourself. Hmm...

Now, I ask you, "Are you creative?"

Take a few moments and list five creative things you have done over the past few weeks, no matter how big or how small:

1.

2.

3.

4.

5.

In case you don't know it by now,
YOU ARE CREATIVE. Congratulations!

~18~
LET'S PLAY "WHAT IF?"

"He who knows others is wise.
He who knows himself is enlightened."
—Lao Tzu

Our creativity is often stifled when we accept norms as our guides to decision-making. For example, you do something a certain way because that's the way it has always been done. But sometimes the old way is best and sometimes it isn't. In this section, I want you to think about a situation in which you need to propose and follow through with a recommended action.

Take a moment and describe the situation:

Now, list the action you recommended and why you selected this alternative.

What other alternatives did you consider? Please list them below and explain why you did not use them.

Now that you have hindsight on the matter, would you have selected another alternative? If so, why? If not, why not?

The important thing about this exercise is that it will help you realize that you are capable of creating many solutions to a problem. Understanding this creative process will help you make clearer choices about your career path. For example, if you determined in the exercise above that the choice you made was to please others at the risk of hurting yourself, you will want to keep this tendency in mind.

~19~
SKILLS, SKILLS AND YES... MORE SKILLS!

"The human mind, once stretched to a new idea,
never goes back to its original dimension."
—*Oliver Wendell Holmes*

We've spent a lot of time exploring creativity as a skill because it is one that overlaps with other skills. Based on my own experiences, I've created the following as some of the most valued employee (and life) skills:

Listening
Organization
Facilitation
Communication
Observation
Ability to research
Assertiveness
Creativity (trying to hide in the middle of the list!)
Openness
Logic/analytical skills
Interpersonal skills
Mindfulness
Intentional
Visualization
Gratitude

Listening skills are critical to understanding the perspectives of others. But more importantly, the ability to listen to ourselves helps guide us in the right direction.

Organization brings clarity and crispness to what you do. Once you have a system for organizing in place, it frees you to do the more fun and creative thinking in your life.

Do you like to "get people talking" and working together to arrive at new and creative solutions to work and home issues? Are you the person expected to "facilitate" these discussions? Maybe you are a Facilitator....

A good communicator provides information in a clear and timely way to the people who need it most. If you are a good communicator, you are skilled at getting the word out to the right people in an efficient way.

Can you pick up little pieces of information just by observing others and the situations they are in? Are you observant about yourself in new and different situations? If so, you know how to use your powers of observation to learn, adapt, and survive in different circumstances. That's a very useful skill in any career today!

Do you enjoy delving into a situation in an attempt to get all of the facts? Do you want to understand the reasons for certain happenings and how something works? Investigative skills and a results orientation are key qualities of someone who is a researcher.

Over the years, have you learned to establish *boundaries for yourself?* In situations when someone is trying to push you too hard, are you able to say no and maintain your comfort zone? As many of us mature, we learn to establish priorities and boundaries, holding true to them no matter how many people try to re-establish them for us. Assertive behavior helps us stay focused on our goals.

New ideas for new situations and new ways of handling old situations are the results of a creative mind. Creativity lifts us to new heights and challenges—it is important to showcase your creative abilities whenever possible.

Openness often goes hand in hand with creativity. If you are open to many solutions to one problem, or willing to consider new opportunities, your chances for success in your chosen career are greater.

Are you a systematic planner who carefully identifies each detailed step in a process? Do you rely on analytical skills to meet your work and home obligations? These are great skill sets.

Interpersonal skills address your ability to relate to others as well as yourself. Understanding yourself and others in the world of work makes life easier.

Are you able to see the big picture? Do you tend to go for the concepts as you begin new projects at home or work?

Conceptualizing roughs out your direction... you can fill in the details later.

We have included the ability to visualize as yet another important skill. Do you look ahead, visualize your goals, and remain focused?

Finally, the ability to be grateful for your experiences, relationships, and lessons along the way is a skill that helps you maintain balance in your life as you move to new and exciting challenges.

Take a moment and, from the list of skills reviewed earlier in this chapter (or others you would like to add), identify your skills and write a personal example of each. You are now on your way to a personal skills inventory.

1. SKILL_____

PERSONAL SKILLS INVENTORY:

2. SKILL_____

PERSONAL SKILLS INVENTORY:

3. SKILL_____

PERSONAL SKILLS INVENTORY:

4. SKILL_____
PERSONAL SKILLS INVENTORY:

5. SKILL_____
PERSONAL SKILLS INVENTORY:

Please list as many skills as you wish, but try to prioritize your top five skills.

Perhaps you want to continue complimenting yourself. Your unique greatness is continuing to surface more and more.

~20~
IDENTIFYING YOUR TALENTS

---

*"The bravest thing you can do
when you are not brave,
is to profess courage and act accordingly."*
—Cora Harris

You may not realize it, but you've already taken many steps forward on your career path. The skills and talents you have developed and enjoyed over the years can lead you in significant directions. The key now is to identify those talents and figure out what they mean for your future.

The next few chapters will help you become aware of the steps you have already taken and provide guidance about where to go from here. Over the years, you have developed many general skills. The last few chapters help you identify the talents and general skills that bring satisfaction to your life.

Perhaps you are best at providing order and structure around the activities of your life. Or maybe you like to find ways to make life more exciting. Whatever the skills are, please keep them in mind as they relate to your evolving career path. Now for the specifics...

~21~

PIECE BY PIECE

---

*"Simplicity of character is the
natural result of profound thought."*
—Thomas Hazlitt

The next few chapters will discuss how you can build specific skills that will expand your career opportunities. They will help you move beyond your general skill set and identify forums in which you can build a set of more specific skills.

Keep in mind that attitude is a key player in developing your plan for skill building. You can either shine light on your possibilities or shroud your dreams in darkness. The choice is yours.

LEARNING ON YOUR TERMS

As you proceed with your career plan, it's important to determine the education/training you need to achieve your goals.

Clearly, some careers require formal undergraduate and graduate school degrees. However, other careers require shorter-term degrees such as associate degrees (two years) or certification programs (six months to one year).

In some careers, solid experience and commitment to a career are the most important credentials for success.

~22~
IF I CAN SEE IT, I CAN GET THERE!

"The invariable mark of wisdom
is to see the miraculous in the common."
—R. W. Emerson

CAREER MAPPING

In this section, I will introduce you to the process of creating a map of your career opportunities. This unique process allows you to refine your career choices as you go along. By the end, your career path will be more apparent.

Start by identifying all of your career possibilities. Don't hold back. Draw upon your general skills (as identified in earlier exercises), your specific interests, related skills, natural talents, and your various fields of interest. Don't worry that you are exploring too many directions at once.

Once you have listed your alternatives, you can create a matrix (format is provided) that will guide you to the path or paths that feel right for you.

This exercise is a great way to affirm your skills and visualize your opportunities. It also "gets the juices flowing" and usually leads to even more ideas about possible careers and how to achieve them. The following example will give you a better idea of what I'm talking about.

THE STORY OF LYNN

Lynn has narrowed her primary interests to law or medicine. Within the field of medicine, she thinks she wants to work with animals more than with people. Lynn loves animals and particularly enjoys working with creatures who appear to need love and attention.

Here's a little background on Lynn. She is in her mid-40s. Her children are off to college and she wants to enter the workforce with a career that will be interesting and challenging.

Lynn has a bachelor's degree in elementary education. She taught for two years after college, then became a stay-at-home mother. Over the past 20 years, she has held leadership roles in her church and her children's schools. She has also been involved in organizations that advocate for children's and animals' rights.

In general, Lynn wants a job where she's helping others, whether it be people or animals. She also wants direct contact with her clients so she can feel closer to the real issues and the solutions she hopes to create.

Now that you know a little about Lynn, let's take a look at her career options. I'm going to organize her possibilities by three categories:

1. Traditional approach
2. Mixed approach
3. Mentoring

As explained earlier, *traditional* approaches are formal education centered. Specific jobs in this category usually require bachelor's, graduate, and/or doctorate degrees.

Under the *mixed* approach, some education is required, but usually this education focuses on developing specific skills for the job.

Finally, *mentoring* suggests that experience is your primary teacher. With a strong mentor, you will be able to step directly into your field of interest, get your feet wet and find out if the choice feels right for you. Let's work through the following career matrix:

CAREER MAP

	LAW	*VETERINARY MEDICINE*	*GENERAL MEDICINE*
TRADITIONAL	Lawyer	Veterinarian	Doctor
MIXED	Paralegal	Vet Assistant	Allied Health
MENTORING	Children's Rights	Kennel Advocate Assistant	Medical Insurance Translator

Under each of these approaches, a job title list is formed. The list can be as short or as long as you wish. Under the heading of Law, for example, Lynn could list lawyer, judge, and law professor under traditional approaches. Under mixed approach, Lynn could expand her list to include law enforcement officer and parole officer. For mentoring, Lynn's interests in preservation of children's rights and animal rights surfaced with her choices of activist and lobbyist. She could also list legal aid counselor for the poor.

ASK THE EXPERTS

As you see, Lynn has many options. In fact, she was so excited after we created this chart, she took my recommendation to talk to people who were involved in specific careers of which she was thinking of pursuing so they could tell her more about the field. She spoke to lawyers, paralegals, rights activists, and lobbyists.

I strongly encourage this type of networking (examples include LinkedIn and other social networks). It helps people understand their fields of interest and leads to information about emerging careers within these fields. Networking obviously helps build contacts that prove useful when you're ready to job hunt.

Don't be shy about reaching out and making these contacts. Most people are more than happy to answer questions about their careers. I have seen such positive responses over the years that I recommend that you take advantage of these opportunities.

The next section of the map is the skills/characteristics list as it pertains to the listed career choices.

GENERAL SKILLS

Through our work together, Lynn was able to focus on her general skills and interests. Lynn sees herself as a critical thinker. She likes to analyze problems and brainstorm solutions.

In addition, she loves to interact with others and she finds that many people respond well to her ideas and participation. Consequently, Lynn ranks her communication and interpersonal skills very high.

Lynn has strong feelings about completing projects that she starts. She is challenged by deadlines and takes pride in meeting them.

She also has a highly developed social conscience. Over the years, she has served in a number of organizations that support the interests of children and animals.

IDEAS AND CHOICES

The next areas of the career map provide ideas on what specific skills are necessary, how much formal education is required, next steps or questions to explore, and some conclusions about each direction.

Let's say Lynn chooses to be a lawyer. In order to achieve this goal, Lynn would need to go to law school for three years. Through interviews and research, she also learned that many of the specific skills of a lawyer suit her. She is analytical, determined, and dedicated. Other aspects of lawyering, especially the highly structured nature of the work, didn't appeal to her as much.

Lynn asked herself the following questions:

- Do I want to go to law school for three years? Will my social responsibility needs be met?

- Will it seem like I am in touch with the service I want to provide?

From the questions, she concluded the following:

- I want to work as soon as possible. I do not want to wait until I achieve a law degree.

- I don't want to think in a box.

- I cannot afford law school at this time. Perhaps I will take a class at a later time.

In contrast, let's take a look at Lynn's findings for rights activist/lobbyist for children/animals:

Through interviews and from her experience with volunteer organizations, Lynn learned she was ready to jump into this field without any additional formal education. There were many aspects of the work she liked, and she would be able to use her problem-solving and communication skills to make a difference.

She considered a few options. She could form an organization to support her public service goals or she could write a column or article to increase public awareness of children/animal issues.

Lynn concluded that she would like to learn to write grants to support her interests in protecting/supporting children's rights.

PRIMARY OBJECTIVE

Lynn created a primary objective based on her newfound knowledge. She reaffirmed her mission to serve others and create direct contact with those she serves. In addition, she concluded that an important objective for her is to continue to explore ideas and opportunities to reach her goals. In other words, she would stay open to many possibilities.

IMPLEMENTATION

Lynn's career map led her to several ideas on implementing her plan. She listed the following:

- Brainstorm with organizations that support children's rights. What needs are not being met in the community?

- How can I make a difference? Where will I obtain funding?

- Continue to refine my plan as I get more information!

Lynn's career map led to some important conclusions about her direction. But more importantly, it affirmed her passion for preserving children's rights.

YOUR TURN

Following are copies of blank career maps. Choose your fields of interest. At this point, try not to exceed three. Complete the forms as shown in the example of Lynn. Do not limit yourself... list your interests and possibilities. As you work through this process, you will naturally narrow down your goals. Each step you take is one step closer for you to experience harmony in your career and in your soul.

The career mapping process highlights that you have more to offer than your work experience. In the next few chapters, I'm going to give you another tool ... a holistic resume that presents all of your skills and talents—not just the ones you gained from a formal education or job. But first, enjoy working on your career maps. The following checklist will help keep you on track during the career mapping process.

CAREER MAPPING CHECKLIST

- ☐ List your career possibilities: explore career options at different forms of education/training (traditional, mixed, and mentoring)
- ☐ List how your general skills and natural talents will support your career possibilities. Is there a career that will more fully utilize your skills versus another?
- ☐ Make arrangements to meet with people who are working in your selected areas of career interest in order to help refine your interests and shape your understanding of your career choices.
- ☐ Based on your discussions with the experts and your research, list the specific skills and education you need to acquire to pursue your career interests.
- ☐ Ask yourself questions about your choices thus far. What feels right about these choices? What does not feel right?
- ☐ What conclusions can you make at this point? Which options seem to "fit" the best?
- ☐ Summarize your understanding of your direction with a primary objective.
- ☐ List your ideas on how you will implement your decision.

(See chart on following pages)

CAREER MAP

Field of Interest:

Approaches

TRADITIONAL
Job Titles

MIXED
Job Titles

MENTORING
Job Titles

General Skills & Natural Talents

Ask the Experts

Interview #1:
Specific skills / Education requirements: ----------------------►

Interview #2:
Specific skills / Education requirements: ----------------------►

Interview #3:
Specific skills / Education requirements: ----------------------►

Self-questions

Interview #1:

Next steps:

Interview #2:

Next steps:

Interview #3:

Next steps:

CONCLUSIONS: INTERVIEW #1

CONCLUSIONS: INTERVIEW #2

CONCLUSIONS: INTERVIEW #3

Primary Objective

Implementation Ideas/Plans

~23~
A MORE COMPLETE YOU ON PAPER

---

*"Man's main task in life
is to give birth to himself."*
—Erich Fromm

Now that you have recognized all the unique skills that make you a very special person, we're going to make connections between those skills, your interests, and your career and life objectives.

Have you ever thought about why so many people dread writing their resumes? I think it is because they dislike the thought of squeezing all of their depth, dimension, and learning into the straightjacket of a typical resume. Ask someone to read their resume to you sometime. Sounds a little robotic, doesn't it?

Webster's Dictionary defines "resume" as to hold, maintain, keep, and continue. Traditional resumes will certainly help you do this.

But if that's what you really wanted to do, I don't think you would be reading this book.

Traditional resumes emphasize formal achievements in the workplace. They are a perfectly fitting way to show where you have been in terms of your work experience, but they ignore other valuable experiences that might be useful in the new job/career you seek.

It's true that most resumes include "incidentals" like outside activities and interests, but this information tends to fall at the bottom of the page. More importantly, the traditional resume doesn't leave room to show your vision and goals and how you intend to go about getting there.

That's not good enough. A resume that shows only a small slice of you may lead to only a small slice of the career you truly want.

~24~

RESUME IN MOTION

"To know one's self is to assert one's self."
—Albert Camus

Okay, it's time to get creative with your resume. The following exercises will help you get there.

Before we start, I want you to remember that your resume is about you. It should look the way you want and be used in a way that makes you feel comfortable.

Perhaps you will use it as a personal assessment of where you have been and a map of where you would like to go. In that case, I suggest that you review it every few months to see what you have accomplished and update the document if necessary.

Under some circumstances, you may feel comfortable showing this document to a prospective employer as an addendum to your traditional resume. Or maybe you will use it as your sole form of communicating your achievements and career goals to a potential employer. The choice is yours and may vary with each case.

PAINTBRUSH TO PAPER

The major components of the resume we will create are as follows:

- ☐ Goal
- ☐ Experience & education
- ☐ Other pursuits

The presentation of Experience & Education and Other Pursuits is somewhat unusual—they will be presented simultaneously, with Experience & Education on the left side of the page and Other Pursuits on the right.

The information on both sides of the page is classified under such characteristics, selected by you, as:

- ☐ Creativity
- ☐ Leadership
- ☐ Vision
- ☐ Growth-oriented
- ☐ Teamwork

Please keep this general information in mind as we proceed through sections of the sample resume.

The chart on the following page shows the format with categories only to help you visualize the flow.

HOLISTIC RESUME FORMAT
KEY INFORMATION

Name:
Address:
Telephone:
E-Mail:

Goal:

EXPERIENCE & EDUCATION   ## OTHER PURSUITS

Accomplishments   Accomplishments

Example of Creativity   **Creativity**   Example of Creativity

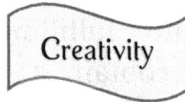

Example of Leadership   **Leadership**   Example of Leadership

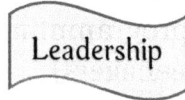

Example of Vision   **Vision**   Example of Vision

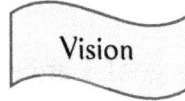

Example of Growth   **Growth**   Example of Growth

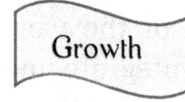

Example of Teamwork   **Teamwork**   Example of Teamwork

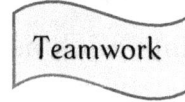

WITH ONE GOAL IN MIND

As you can see, the resume begins with basic information like your name and address.

The next step is the presentation of your goal. As the following example shows, the idea is to provide a broad summary of your goal and specific insights and directions you would like to take.

Lance Richards

378 Paxton Street
Philadelphia, PA 19501

GOAL: Combine education, work experience and natural talents to achieve greater purpose and fulfillment in my career. Specifically, obtain a position in strategic planning/creative direction in education television programming for young viewers (children/teenagers).

As you can see from the goal, Lance wants a position that will value his education and experiences as well as his achievements outside of the world of work. In other words, he hopes to integrate most of the skills and interests that have made him the person he is today.

Specifically, Lance wants a job as a strategic planner/ creative director in educational television programming for young viewers. As you proceed through this resume, you will get a better understanding of Lance's talents and background and why this goal is a strong career fit for him.

EXPERIENCE/EDUCATION & OTHER PURSUITS

As mentioned earlier, Experience & Education and Other Pursuits are listed together in this section, as shown on the following page. The Experience portion includes very basic information: jobs held over the past ten years, where the positions were held, and duration. The Education section lists schools, degrees achieved, and timing of graduation.

You will see on the following page how education and work experience are expanded upon per the characteristics (e.g., creativity) we mentioned earlier. Please review the Experience & Education sections.

EXPERIENCE & EDUCATION
Finance Manager (5 years)
Major Corporation
Philadelphia, PA 19501

M.B.A.   University of Pennsylvania
                Philadelphia, PA

B.A.   Business Administration
                Temple University, Philadelphia, PA

OTHER PURSUITS
Writer: Member of the following writers groups:

- Temple University Fiction Writers Group
  Philadelphia, PA
- Rittenhouse Square Writers Group
  Philadelphia, PA

Contributed several short stories to group for review and critique. ♦ Received very positive feedback. ♦ Currently seeking publication of selected stories.

Teacher:

- "Finance Workshops"
  Major Corporation
- "Reading and Interpreting Financial Statements"
  The Penn State University

Create new and interesting ways to acquaint non-finance professionals with finance fundamentals ♦ Rely on games, exercises, and team involvement to reduce fear of number/ formulas, and to encourage understanding of finance concepts.

Artist: Drawing/Tile block prints

In addition, other pursuits are provided that highlight Lance's interests and experiences outside his traditional work environment. He has pursued writing and teaching and is also an artist in several mediums.

As a writer, he has several tangible achievements to list in this section. He is or has been a member of two writers groups, submitting stories for review and critique by the group members. And he's in the process of seeking publication for some of his short stories.

Lance has taught at a local university. As a teacher, he has enjoyed conducting workshops. Under this section, he provides his approach and philosophy for teaching this course.

And, finally, as an artist, he highlights his interest in creating drawings and tile block prints.

All of these "other pursuits" have added greatly to his development and have prompted him to pursue a career that will allow him to blend more skills from his other pursuits into his work.

CREATIVITY

This portion of the resume highlights Lance's creative abilities and achievements both in terms of his traditional work as well as in his other pursuits. Let's review this section:

EXPERIENCE
Problem solver ♦ Create approaches to develop means of analyzing new strategic opportunities ♦ Challenged by changing needs/abstract thinking ♦ Examples include

evaluation of Major's new product opportunities, white collar productivity measurement, and employee stock ownership education ♦ Old methods no longer apply—find new ways to evaluate new opportunities.

OTHER PURSUITS
Writer of short story fiction ♦ Variety of topics ♦ Character focus and development ♦ Inspired by life and the complexities of people ♦ Creative approach to teaching finance fundamentals ♦ Make it fun for non-finance professionals (games/exercises) ♦ Workshops taught internally at Major and course taught during spring semester at Penn State University

As you can see, Lance has used his work experience to develop his skills as a problem solver and abstract thinker who is open to new ways of getting a job done. Several examples have been listed to highlight his successes.

On the Other Pursuits side of creativity, we gain a better understanding of Lance's creative approach to writing fiction as well as teaching.

LEADERSHIP
This portion of the resume highlights Lance's leadership qualities and accomplishments. In his current position as a manager, he leads by example and encourages participation. His job entails a great deal of responsibility, and he has also worked with the top leadership in his company.

EXPERIENCE

Coach/empower staff of three professionals ◆ Foster teamwork and openness ◆ Lead by example ◆ Participative style ◆ Present results to senior management ◆ Serve as Quality Coordinator for all of finance ◆ Encourage the challenging of norms and foster the excitement of finding new and better ways to achieve goals

OTHER PURSUITS

Lead self to new challenges and opportunities—enjoy the process along the way ◆ Foster characteristics such as openness, understanding, persistence, and resourcefulness ◆ Continue to pursue writing opportunities ◆ Make contributions to the community (e.g., serve as tutor at Literacy Council) ◆ Commitment to exercise and good health

Lance enjoys challenges. As a leader, he works to be open, understanding, and resourceful. His near-term personal leadership goals are to continue to focus on teaching via writing and the classroom and to serve the community wherever it is appropriate.

VISION

Vision is an important characteristic for anyone who wants to meet the challenge of change in their environment. As the Experience side below shows, Lance works at anticipating future needs of the company, and developing himself and his staff to meet these business needs.

In terms of his Other Pursuits, he continues to pursue opportunities to use his creative talents and abilities. In other words, his vision correlates strongly to his motivation to grow and find a better career fit.

EXPERIENCE
Anticipate changes in company culture and prepare staff accordingly ◆ Maximize resources to meet business needs

OTHER PURSUITS
Pursue opportunities that enable me to combine my experience and creative endeavors ◆ Continually refine the definition of "purpose" relative to my work

GROWTH ORIENTED

In this section, we learn that in his current job, Lance has a history of adopting new methods of analysis to get the job done. He also seeks new projects to continue to grow his skill base. On the Other Pursuits side of things, he describes himself as a perpetual learner and avid reader who likes to explore and is open to new ways to grow.

EXPERIENCE
Adopt new methods for analysis where appropriate ◆ Actively seek new project opportunities among company population.

94

OTHER PURSUITS
Open to new ways to grow ◆ Avid reader ◆ Passionate about learning ◆ Curious ◆ Explorer

TEAMWORK
The last important quality on this resume is the ability to work well with teams. Lance's resume shows that he has frequently volunteered himself, and his team, for a variety of assignments. On the Other Pursuits side of things, he shows that his participation in writers groups has provided another outlet for teamwork, as he relies on group members to help him improve his short stories.

EXPERIENCE
Participative style ◆ Volunteer myself and staff for team opportunities

OTHER PURSUITS
Participate in two writers groups ◆ Critique and appreciate work of others ◆ Enjoy the benefits of team relationships/dynamics as part of the learning process

THE TOTAL PICTURE
The next two pages present the total resume as discussed above. It is helpful to see the complete format as you

think about how you might structure a similar resume. Here are a few things to keep in mind as you create this resume.

The purpose of the resume is to help you present *all* of your major skills, and natural talents, not just the ones you learned on the job. Give yourself the time to be creative with this format. Even if you do not present it to anyone else, presenting it to yourself could be a very rewarding experience.

The characteristics used in this example, such as creativity, leadership, vision, and so on, were selected by Lance because he wanted to emphasize these areas. Obviously, you may select other characteristics and skill sets to highlight. That is up to you.

Take a chance to look at yourself in a new way. All the best to you!

(See example of formatted resume on the following pages.)

LANCE RICHARDS

378 Paxton Street
Philadelphia, PA 19501

Goal: Combine education, work experience, and natural talents to
achieve greater purpose and fulfillment in my career. Specifically, obtain a
position in strategic planning/creative direction in education television
programming for young American viewers (children/teenagers).

♦ **Experience & Education**

Finance Manager (5 years)
Major Corporation
Philadelphia, PA 19501

M.B.A.
University of Pennsylvania
Philadelphia, PA

B.A. Business Admin
Temple University
Philadelphia, PA

Other Pursuits

Writer

Member of:
*Temple University Fiction
Philadelphia, PA

*Rittenhouse Square Writer's Group
Philadelphia, PA

Contributed several short stories for
review and critique ♦ Received very
positive feedback ♦ Currently
seeking publication of selected
stories

Teacher

"Finance Workshops"
Major Corporation

"Reading & Interpreting Financial
Statements"
The Penn State University

Create new and interesting ways to
acquaint non-finance professionals
with finance fundamentals ♦ Rely
on games, exercises, and team
involvement to reduce fear of
numbers/formulas, and to
encourage understanding of finance
concepts

CREATIVITY

Problem solver ◆ Create approaches to develop means of analyzing new strategic opportunities ◆ Challenged by changing needs/abstract thinking ◆ Examples include evaluation of Major's new product opportunities, white collar productivity measurement, and employee stock ownership education ◆ Old methods no longer apply—find new ways to evaluate new opportunities

Artist

Participate in two writers groups ◆ Critique and appreciate work of others ◆ Enjoy the benefits of team relationships/dynamics as part of the learning process

LEADERSHIP

Coach/empower staff of three professionals ◆ Foster teamwork and openness ◆ Lead by example ◆ Participative style ◆ Present results to senior management ◆ Serve as Quality Coordinator for all of finance ◆ Encourage the challenging of norms and foster the excitement of finding new and better ways to achieve goals

Lead self to new challenges and opportunities and enjoy the process along the way ◆ Foster characteristics such as openness, understanding, persistence, and resourcefulness ◆ Continue to pursue writing opportunities ◆ Make contributions to the community (e.g., serve as tutor at Literacy Council) ◆ Commitment to exercise and good health.

VISION

Anticipate changes in company culture and prepare staff accordingly ◆ Maximize resources to meet business needs

Pursue opportunities that enable me to combine my experience and creative endeavors ◆ Continually refine the definition of "purpose" relative to my work

GROWTH

Adopt new methods for analysis where appropriate ♦ Actively seek new project opportunities among company

Open to new ways to grow ♦ Avid reader ♦ Passionate about learning ♦ Curious ♦ Explorer.

TEAMWORK

Participative style ♦ Volunteer myself and staff for team opportunities

Participate in two writers groups ♦ Critique and appreciate work of others ♦ Enjoy the benefits of team relationships/dynamics as part of the learning process

~25~
ROLL 'EM

"True life is lived when tiny changes occur."
—Leo Tolstoy

Now it's time to get your plan rolling. The most important part of following through on your plan is to break it down into steps that are challenging but are not going to scare you into a permanent retreat. It is important that you are fair to yourself throughout this process and give yourself the time you need to prepare for each step. At the same time, you must be your own cheerleader along the way. It is so important to give yourself credit for each victory!

THE STORY OF KELLY

Let's look at the story of a teacher, Kelly, who always wanted to be a writer. Kelly always felt she had a calling to write but the thought of writing and sharing her material was overwhelming and scary. What would happen if she shared her work too early and critics told her she had no talent for writing stories?

For a long time, Kelly did not pursue her dream because she was not ready to develop a plan and take steps toward developing her creative writing ability.

When she actually did begin her journey into writing, about ten years ago, she knew she had to do it on her terms—nobody else really needed to know of her plan.

She began writing in a journal, with her entries taking on a different form each day. Some days she simply wrote an account of her day and how she felt about it. Other days, she wrote poetry or crafted song lyrics.

The journal became a great outlet for her feelings and creativity. It was one place she could go without feeling any limitations. She gained confidence as she read old entries and saw the progress she had made.

After a few years of journal writing, story ideas began to pop into Kelly's head. Titles, characters, settings, and a variety of situations began to flow. Kelly outlined several stories in her head and started to outline them in her journal.

Soon Kelly joined a local writers group to compare notes with other writers and get a better understanding of the craft of story writing.

Kelly was terrified the first time she shared her stories with writing group members, but she received positive feedback and was strongly encouraged to continue on the path she had developed for herself.

I want to make a few general points about Kelly's story. Kelly began her writing in a very personal way... a way that made sense for her.

While she was exploring her writing abilities, Kelly was busy with other demanding activities such as work and family life. It is safe to say that she eased himself into the world of writing, yet this schedule worked well for her, and she had support along the way.

~26~
VISUALIZE AND REALIZE

"We cannot control the wind,
but we can control our sails."
—Anon

Before you realize your achievements, it is important to be able to visualize them. If you can see your desired outcome, it becomes easier to see yourself getting there.

Better yet, immerse yourself in your dream and it will become part of your life.

Close your eyes and envision your future as much as possible! The more you live this way, the more doors will open to help you find your way. New ways of getting to where you want to be will become more apparent. And, these doors lead to new doors, and so on. In short, live in constant belief and stay open.

As you move toward your goals, try to avoid negative forces. Take good care of yourself with exercise, rest, and a healthy diet. Surround yourself with positive- thinking people.

~27~

UP THE TEMPO

"I create my own security
by trusting the process of life."
—Louise L. Hay

Not progressing fast enough? Remember, you are in charge of your career path. If you are getting discouraged because you are not getting to your goal fast enough, it is up to you to make things happen.

Here are some ideas:

Challenge yourself more often. If you are ready for your next step, proceed. Surround yourself with others interested in similar goals. Usually input, knowledge, and ideas shared with other positive-thinking, pro-active people will present additional steps to move you toward your goals in more depth and precision.

Establish daily, weekly, and monthly goals. Give yourself a pep talk and renew your energy related to the pursuit of your goal. Intensity can propel you toward your goal by keeping you more focused.

Again, it is even more important to *take very good care of yourself at this time*! Exercise, a healthy diet, and relaxation are self-care essentials. You are using a lot of energy!

~28~
WRONG IS RIGHT

---

*"No trumpets sound when the important
decisions of our life are made;
destiny is made known silently."*
—Agnes DeMille

Often, to refine your career path, you need to break away from traditional models and create ways of exploring and defining what suits you best.

I view career pathing as an adventure. Even though you may have spent a lot of time plotting your direction, you are bound to take a wrong turn now and then. You might find yourself in a situation where you say, "This is not for me." That's the time to stop and refine your path... not to give up!

In one sense, there is no such thing as a wrong turn because if a bump in the road causes you to refine your career path, you will ultimately gain more focus and direction.

You're also likely to experience some unexpected successes. Use these miraculous experiences as guides toward further refinement of your career path. In other words, as you progress toward your career goal, stay open to both victories and defeats. They will serve as touchstones to move you toward greater fulfillment.

Make sure you give yourself the time you need—it will save time and effort in the long run.

~29~
AN ENDING AND A BEGINNING

---

*"Too many people overvalue what they are not
and undervalue what they are."*
—*Malcolm Forbes*

"I learned this at least... that if one advances confidently in the direction of his dreams and endeavors to live the life which he has imagined...

He will meet with a success unexpected in common hours. He will put some things behind.

Will pass an invisible boundary.

New, universal, and more liberal laws will begin to establish themselves around and within him, as the old laws are expanded...

And he will live with the license of a higher order of beings."

—*Thoreau*

ADVANCE CONFIDENTLY

To "advance confidently," it's important to understand the power within you. A consistent belief in yourself and your possibilities holds you to your path and strengthens your ability to take the sometimes difficult steps toward growth and fulfillment.

The following phrases illustrate my definition of the power within:

- I'm responsible.
- Life's an adventure.
- I am alive with possibility.
- Life's an opportunity.
- I will try!
- I feel myself growing stronger.
- It is all happening perfectly.
- I am confident and self-assured.
- I will share my positive attitude with all who touch my life.

As you create and experience these feelings, you will present yourself to others in a very positive and confident way.

One other way to achieve some of these feelings is to allow yourself to use words that suggest the power within—words that show you are in control and will help them realize your goals. Here are some examples of the gentle power words that convey your inner strength:

Compassion	Courage	Integrity
Appreciation	Responsible	Simplicity
Respect	Proactive	Vision
Accountable	Flexible	Focus
Optimism	Grateful	Sensitivity
Honesty	Passion	Openness

Keep these statements in mind on your path to your dreams.

~30~
No More Waiting for an Evolution

"The present moment is filled
with joy and happiness.
If you are attentive, you will see it."
—Thich Nhat Hanh

You have read every chapter in this book. You have completed the exercises in each chapter. You have a better understanding of where you have been and where you are going in your career.

You know more of who you are. You see more clearly your special strengths. You are more aware of your possibilities. You are no longer waiting for what you will become... you are in charge of your evolution.

Define. Grow. Refine. Grow. Refine further. Evolve.

Congratulations!

TODAY & TOMORROW

You have taken a good look at who you are as well as the skills and talents you have to offer. You have established goals that will help you move along your career path and refine your position in the world of work. Be aware of your uniqueness and give yourself credit. Be grateful for you!

Many people never take such steps. They wait and hope that the right job will suddenly appear. If it does not happen, they rationalize that somehow they were not worthy of better opportunities.

You have chosen not to live and work this way. You have taken a position of power that will lead to the comfort and peace that being proactive, not a victim, can provide.

In summary of all that you have learned, included is a seven-step awareness checklist to keep in mind as you embark on this process and as a refresher as you proceed.

SEVEN-STEP AWARENESS CHECKLIST

Awareness of:

- Self... thoughts and feelings about your career and your life
- Your dreams and your special areas of interest
- Natural talents—acknowledgment and true acceptance of those talents
- General skills
- Top five career and life priorities
- Two or three career fields to explore
- An action plan

Reading this book and working through the exercises is very hard work. I'm sure you had periods of exhaustion and confusion. Completing this book, however, should give you feelings of energy and empowerment.

Congratulations on your accomplishments!

Along the way, I have known...

- Administrative assistants who have become teachers
- Teachers who have become accountants
- Accountants who have become artists
- An executive who became a writer

And you will become a .... ?

The above passage is to help remind you of all that you have accomplished. Read it again and again and reward yourself for the steps you have taken.

~31~
THE HIGH ROAD

---

*"Life is either a daring adventure
or nothing at all."*
—Helen Keller

The high road is the perfect route to your destination. The high road is paved with ideas, optimism, vision, openness, fairness, sensitivity, spirit, and initiative.

Be patient with yourself.

Be gentle with yourself.

Be grateful for all that you have—your talents, your skills, and your kindness.

Give accolades to you! You are great! Go ahead, live the life that you imagine!

Follow your Authentic Path...

Experience your *Harmony!!*

Definition...

HARMONY:

~ Balance

~ Accord

~Agreement

~PEACE

ABOUT THE AUTHOR

Professional and personal coach DONNA R. STYER is owner and president of D. R. Styer and Associates, a central Pennsylvania-based firm that works with individuals, management teams, and corporations to create dramatic changes in interpersonal skills, work/life balance, and leadership. Donna's exuberance for transforming businesses and individuals has created a successful career as professional coach and management consultant to the corporate world and private clients for over 25 years.

With a keen insight into asking the right questions, Donna has been a synergist for positive change in corporations such as Chase Manhattan Bank, Kellogg's, Johnson & Johnson, and Armstrong World Industries as well as colleges, small businesses and individual clients. Her innovative, holistic approach encompasses the mental, physical, and emotional obstacles that limit our own, and therefore our organizations, success.

Discover your unique contribution, and make it.

Donna R. Styer is a Master Certified Coach by the International Coach Federation and for several years a member of the Philadelphia Area Coaches Alliances. Based in Lancaster, Pennsylvania, her e-mail address is Coaching@drstyer.org

Ms. Styer's services include:
❑ Executive, Career and Life coaching
❑ Organizational development
❑ Personal enhancement

About the Author

SCOTT McNELIS is an accomplished and forward-thinking finance leader with expertise in the areas of New Product Innovation and Portfolio Management. Throughout his career, he has been dedicated to driving growth while balancing complexity and profitability. He has been very successful navigating challenging projects and collaborating with others to deliver business goals.

In addition to his finance career, Scott is dedicated to sharing his skills as a volunteer for select non-profit organizations. He is passionate about learning and growth and consistently challenges himself with new opportunities.

Scott is also a dedicated father and husband. He is always inspired and motivated by the family he and his wife have created.

www.ingramcontent.com/pod-product-compliance
Lightning Source LLC
Chambersburg PA
CBHW071704210326
41597CB00017B/2326